DINOSAUR WARS

TRICERATOPS

★ ★ ★ ★ ★ ★ ★ ★ ★ ★

VS

STEGOSAURUS

★ ★ ★ ★ ★ ★ ★ ★ ★ ★

WHEN HORNS AND PLATES COLLIDE

Michael O'Hearn

Consultant:
Mathew J. Wedel, PhD
Paleontologist

Raintree

www.raintreepublishers.co.uk
Visit our website to find out
more information about
Raintree books.

To order:
☎ Phone 0845 6044371
🖨 Fax +44 (0) 1865 312263
✉ Email myorders@raintreepublishers.co.uk

Customers from outside the UK please telephone +44 1865 312262

Raintree is an imprint of Capstone Global Library Limited, a company incorporated
in England and Wales having its registered office at 7 Pilgrim Street, London,
EC4V 6LB – Registered company number: 6695582

Text © Capstone Press 2010
First published in hardback in the United Kingdom by Capstone Global Library in 2011
The moral rights of the proprietor have been asserted.

Editors: Aaron Sautter and Laura Knowles
Designer: Kyle Grenz
Media Researcher: Marcie Spence
Art Director: Nathan Gassman
Production Specialist: Laura Manthe
Illustrations by Philip Renne and Jon Hughes
Originated by Capstone Global Library Ltd
Printed and bound in China by South China Printing Company Ltd

ISBN 978 1 406 21820 6 (hardback)
14 13 12 11 10
10 9 8 7 6 5 4 3 2 1

British Library Cataloguing in Publication Data
A full catalogue record for this book is available from the British Library.

Acknowledgements
We would like to thank the following for permission to reproduce photographs: Shutterstock
parchment backgrounds (Valery Potapova), **stylized backgrounds** (Leigh Prather).

Disclaimer
All the Internet addresses (URLs) given in this book were valid at the time of going to press.
However, due to the dynamic nature of the Internet, some addresses may have changed, or
sites may have changed or ceased to exist since publication. While the author and Publishers
regret any inconvenience this may cause readers, no responsibility for any such changes can be
accepted by either the author or the publisher.

CONTENTS

WELCOME TO DINOSAUR WARS!

Dinosaurs were brutal creatures. They fought each other and ate each other. Usually it was meat-eater versus plant-eater or big versus small. But in Dinosaur Wars, it's a free for all. Plant-eaters attack plant-eaters. Giants fight giants. And small dinosaurs gang up on huge opponents. In Dinosaur Wars, any dinosaur battle is possible!

In this dinosaur war, Triceratops and Stegosaurus collide. You'll see how these two plant-eaters could be downright brutal. You'll learn about their defensive abilities. You'll discover their wicked weapons. Although these two dinosaurs usually didn't try to pick fights, you'll find out how they may have brawled. Then you'll see them battling head-to-head – and you'll get to watch from a front row seat!

Triceratops (try-SERRA-tops)
Stegosaurus (STEG-oh-sore-us)

THE
COMBATANTS

TRICERATOPS VS STEGOSAURUS

Triceratops and Stegosaurus never actually butted heads. Stegosaurus lived from about 155 to 144 million years ago, before it died out. That was millions of years before the first Triceratops walked the earth. Triceratops lived from about 67 million years ago until dinosaurs became **extinct** about 65 million years ago.

If Triceratops and Stegosaurus had lived at the same time, they probably would have bumped into each other. Both lived in what is now the western United States. In fact, fossils of both dinosaurs were first discovered in Colorado, USA.

But even if Triceratops and Stegosaurus had met, it's unlikely they would have battled. Both were **herbivores**. Their deadly weapons were used for defence rather than attacking.

Both Triceratops and Stegosaurus were named by scientist Othniel Charles Marsh. Marsh discovered more than 80 species of dinosaurs.

FIERCE FACT
DISCOVERY

extinct no longer living anywhere in the world

herbivore animal that eats only plants

SIZE

Triceratops
9 metres long; 9 tonnes
★ ★ ★ ★

★ ★ ★
Stegosaurus
9 metres long; 2.7 tonnes

At 9 metres (30 feet) long and weighing up to 9 tonnes, Triceratops could bash through whatever got in his way. With his shield-like neck **frill**, Triceratops was built like a bulldozer. Triceratops' size and weight would be a big advantage in a fight.

frill bony collar that fans around an animal's neck

8

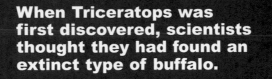

Stegosaurus was about as big as a school bus. He was 9 metres (30 feet) long and weighed about 2.7 tonnes. In the dinosaur world, Stegosaurus was far from being a giant. He was big enough to put up a good fight, but he would have trouble beating a larger opponent.

SPEED AND AGILITY

Triceratops
Fast and powerful
★ ★ ★

★ ★
Stegosaurus
Slow but nimble

Stegosaurus was a clumsy runner. His back legs were twice as long as his front legs. This was not the best design for speed. But it pushed Stegosaurus' weight towards his back end so he could **pivot** quickly on his back legs. This movement helped him keep his mighty spiked tail between him and his enemies.

pivot turn on a central point
evolve develop over a long time with gradual changes

Scientists think both Triceratops and Stegosaurus evolved from dinosaurs that walked on two legs rather than four.

FIERCE FACT
LEGS

Triceratops was built like a rhino. His sturdy legs and broad feet supported his heavy, muscular body. Triceratops ran fast for his size, possibly up to 32 kilometres (20 miles) per hour. However, he could not turn easily. He usually just charged straight ahead. He was built to run into his enemies, not away from them.

WEAPONS

Stegosaurus had only one weapon, but it was deadly. His tail was powerful and dangerous. It had four hard, sharp spikes attached to the end. Each sword-like spike was up to 1 metre (3 feet) long. A swift strike from Stegosaurus' spiked tail could bring death to any opponent.

The name Triceratops means "three–horned face".

Triceratops had spikes of his own. Two horns stuck out above his eyes, and a third was at the tip of his snout. The snout horn was short, but it could cause great damage when crashing into an enemy. The upper horns were long and sharp. They could be driven into an enemy's body. Triceratops also had a sharp, powerful beak. It could deliver a painful bite. Of all the plant-eating dinosaurs, Triceratops was among the most dangerous.

DEFENCES

Triceratops
Bony neck frill
★ ★ ★ ★ ★

★ ★ ★ ★ ★
Stegosaurus
Bony back plates

Triceratops' bony neck frill extended from the top of his head. It acted like a shield to protect the dinosaur's neck. The frill was useful when Triceratops barrelled into an opponent head first. Many fossils of Triceratops frills show battle scars. They prove that the neck frill was a valuable defence. The frill may also have made Triceratops look more dangerous to his enemies.

Stegosaurus' back plates were not attached to the rest of his skeleton.

Stegosaurus had two rows of bony plates running along his back from his neck to his tail. Scientists once thought these plates lay flat on the dinosaur's back like armour. Today, scientists think the back plates stood upright for protection during attacks. The plates may also have helped different **species** tell one another apart.

species group of animals that share common characteristics

15

ATTACK STYLE

Triceratops
Bashing and biting
⭐ ⭐ ⭐

⭐ ⭐ ⭐
Stegosaurus
Powerful tail smash

In a fight, Stegosaurus tried to keep enemies behind him. He moved sideways and in circles to line up opponents for his dangerous tail swing. Stegosaurus' tail was more flexible than the tails of most dinosaurs. He could whip it up and down and from side to side to smash his opponents.

Triceratops kept his enemies in front of him where he could bash and bite them. All of his weapons were attached to his head. He needed to get up close to cause damage. He would charge with his head down to pierce an enemy with his horns. Afterwards, he could bite his opponent with his powerful beak or keep stabbing with his horns.

GET READY TO RUMBLE!

Get ready for the rumble, the boom, and the crash! It's time for the thunder and the pain. These two dinosaurs don't just fight, they bash! In one corner is the mighty bulldozer – Triceratops! He's horned and heavy and ready to charge. In the other corner is the spiky challenger – Stegosaurus! He's a brawler with a deadly tail, and he's not afraid to use it. The winner of this knockout battle is anybody's guess.

TRICERATOPS

★★★★ SIZE

★★★ SPEED AND AGILITY

★★★ WEAPONS

★★★★★ DEFENCES

★★★★ ATTACK STYLE

STEGOSAURUS

You've got a front row seat. So sit back, turn the page, and get ready to enjoy the battle!

ONE LAST THING...

This battle is made up. It's fake. These dinos never fought. And even if they did, no one knows how it would have happened. Nobody knows which dinosaur would have won. But if you like a good battle, this one should be a smash!

THE BATTLE

It's early in the morning. The sky is grey. Swirls of mist hang in the air. Stegosaurus stands at the edge of a clearing, munching on some leaves. He hears something rustling in the bushes nearby. He slowly cranes his neck to look in the direction of the sound. He keeps chewing leaves while staring at some ferns across the clearing.

Ferns are his favourite meal, so Stegosaurus slowly walks towards them. When he gets close, he sees the plants sway back and forth. He hears heavy breathing and a snapping sound.

Stegosaurus ignores the sounds and reaches down for a mouthful of ferns. He takes one bite and then another. Suddenly a giant, horned head pops up from the leafy plants. It's Triceratops, and he isn't happy.

Compared to his size, Stegosaurus' brain was very small. It was about the size of a golf ball.

FIERCE FACT

THE BRAIN

Triceratops charges through the ferns and aims his horns at Stegosaurus. The distance is short, and Triceratops doesn't gather much speed. Stegosaurus tries to back out of the way. But his feet trip over the leafy plants, and he tumbles backwards. He topples to the ground with an earthshaking thud.

Triceratops rumbles to a stop. He watches as Stegosaurus tries to climb to his feet. Stegosaurus' broad side makes a big target. Triceratops charges again. This time he gains speed.

As Triceratops gets closer,
Stegosaurus rolls to his knees.
He doesn't have time to get up
before Triceratops' horns bore into
him. Stegosaurus quickly flops
to his side and whips his spiked
tail at his enemy. One of the tail
spikes stabs right through
Triceratops' bony neck frill.

Some scientists once thought that
Stegosaurus had a second brain. But
it was really a nerve bundle near his
hips that controlled his tail, much
like birds have today.

FIERCE
FACT

TAIL
CONTROL

As Stegosaurus rolls back to his feet, his spike remains stuck in his opponent's frill. Triceratops wails and jerks his massive head from side to side. As he does, he yanks Stegosaurus' tail. Stegosaurus is pulled off balance and lands on his side again.

FIERCE FACT

FOSSILS

Several fossils of meat-eating dinosaurs have holes that match Stegosaurus' tail spikes.

Triceratops' eyes blaze. He charges once more. But this time, he runs away from his opponent. As he bolts, he drags Stegosaurus behind him. Stegosaurus tries to stop his enemy, but he can't find a firm footing. He zigzags and bounces behind Triceratops. Earth and plants are raked up behind the two giant beasts.

Triceratops dashes wildly out of the clearing, trampling through the bushes. He charges through a small stream, slips, and crashes head first to the ground. Stegosaurus tumbles to a stop next to him. Stegosaurus' tail is still lodged in Triceratops' frill. Triceratops opens his sharp beak and bites down hard on his enemy's tail.

Stegosaurus screeches and rips his tail out of Triceratops' beak. Triceratops' head is yanked into the muddy stream bank. Stegosaurus' spike is finally freed.

Stegosaurus climbs to his feet. He lashes wildly with his spikes. He grazes Triceratops' hind leg, ripping open a long, bloody gash. Triceratops bellows. Bloody and angry, Triceratops rises to his feet. He stares furiously at Stegosaurus and backs away. Stegosaurus swipes again with his tail. But the blow doesn't hit – it's just a warning.

The two beasts stare each other down. Triceratops scuffs his heel in the earth and lowers his head. Stegosaurus turns and runs.

Triceratops charges. The ground shakes with each thunderous step. He quickly closes in on the slower Stegosaurus. Triceratops tenses his body for the collision. At the last second, Stegosaurus whips his tail at his attacker. Two long spikes slam into Triceratops' chest. Triceratops crashes to the ground and slides down the muddy stream bank. Stegosaurus pulls out the spikes, leaving two bloody wounds. He stares down at the toppled Triceratops and screeches in victory!

The name Stegosaurus means "roof lizard".

GLOSSARY

evolve develop over a long time with gradual changes

extinct no longer living. An extinct animal is one whose kind has died out completely.

fossil remains or traces of plants and animals that are preserved as rock

frill bony collar that fans out around an animal's neck

herbivore animal that eats only plants

pivot turn on a central point

species group of plants or animals that share common characteristics

FIND OUT MORE

BOOKS

Dinosaur Encyclopedia, Caroline Bingham
  (Dorling Kindersley, 2007)

Dinosaur Hunters: Palaeontologists, Louise and
  Richard Spilsbury (Heinemann Library, 2007)

Prehistoric Scary Creatures, John Malam
  (Book House, 2008)

WEBSITE

www.nhm.ac.uk/kids-only/dinosaurs
Visit the Natural History Museum's website to discover
more than 300 types of dinosaur, play dinosaur games,
and find out what sort of dinosaur you would be!

PLACES TO VISIT

Dinosaur Isle
Sandown, Isle of Wight PO36 8QA
www.dinosaurisle.com

Natural History Museum
London SW7 5BD
www.nhm.ac.uk

The Dinosaur Museum
Dorchester DT1 1EW
www.thedinosaurmuseum.com

INDEX